OFFICIAL

FORTNITE

BATTLE JOURNAL

WILDFIRE

HEADLINE PUBLISHING GROUP
An Hachette UK Company
Carmelite House
50 Victoria Embankment
London, EC4 0DZ
www.headline.co.uk   www.hachette.co.uk

Little, Brown and Company
Hachette Book Group
1290 Avenue of the Americas, New York, NY 10104
Visit us at LBYR.com

www.epicgames.com

First Edition: April 2019

First U.S. Edition: May 2019

Little, Brown and Company is a division of Hachette Book Group, Inc.

The Little, Brown name and logo are trademarks of Hachette Book Group, Inc.

The publisher is not responsible for websites (or their content) that are not owned by the publisher.

ISBN: 978-0-316-42517-9 (pbk.)

Printed in the United States of America
All images © Epic Games, Inc.

WOR
Hardcover: 10 9 8 7 6 5 4 3 2 1
Paperback: 10 9 8 7 6 5 4 3 2 1

CONTENTS

DEAR FORTNITE FAN,

Welcome to your Fortnite Battle Journal! As you know, there is no right or wrong way to play this game. You can master the tips and tricks, but ultimately the joy of Fortnite is that you'll be up against something new every time—and what matters most is developing your own strategy, unique to you.

This logbook will keep you up to date with your progress as you play: You can see it as a chance to keep a record of the loot you've picked up along the way, to stay on top of your daily stats and tactics, or to remind yourself of your most legendary battles and what it took to win them.

Whether you're just starting out on your Fortnite adventure or already have a few hundred Battle Royales behind you, use this logbook to track your results, refine your style, hone your skills, and figure out what's worked best for YOU.

P.S. Don't forget to turn to the "In the Locker" section at the back for more space to harness your creativity and record your latest Fortnite goals!

THE BATTLE JOURNAL

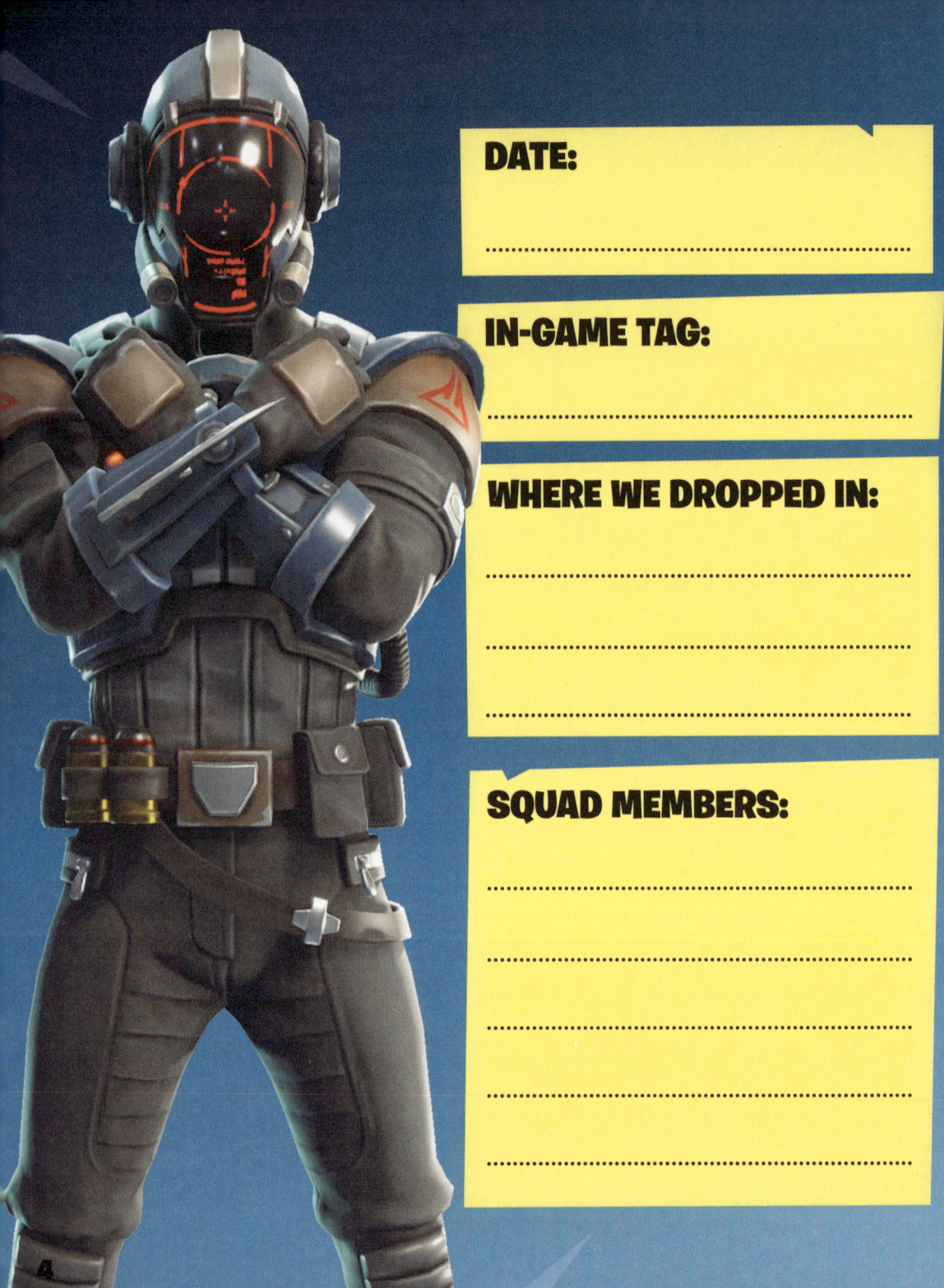

DATE:

....

IN-GAME TAG:

....

WHERE WE DROPPED IN:

....

....

....

SQUAD MEMBERS:

....

....

....

....

....

LOCKER:

OUTFIT

....

BACK BLING

....

PICKAXE

....

TRAIL

....

EMOTES

....

LOADOUT:

....

....

....

....

....

TACTICS:

....

....

....

....

....

KEY STATS:

TOTAL ELIMINATIONS IN ONE GAME

....

TOTAL ELIMINATIONS FOR THE DAY

....

FINAL PLACEMENTS

....

VICTORY ROYALES EARNED:

....

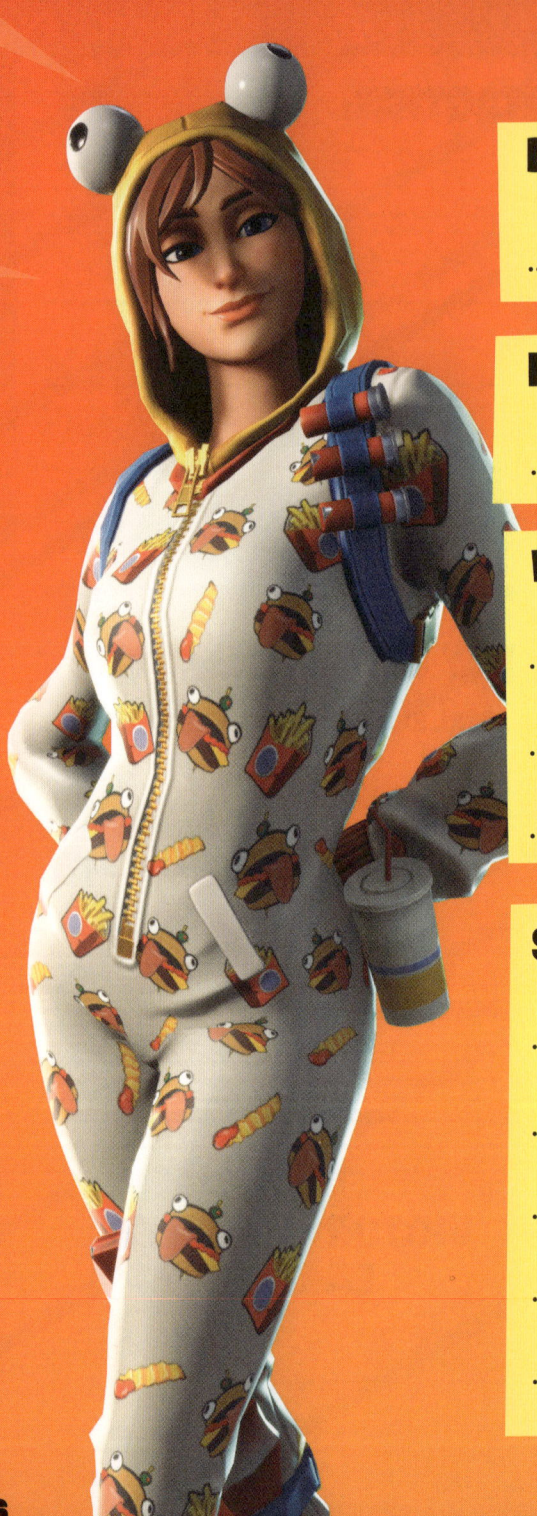

DATE:

....

IN-GAME TAG:

....

WHERE WE DROPPED IN:

....

....

....

SQUAD MEMBERS:

....

....

....

....

....

LOCKER:

OUTFIT

....

BACK BLING

....

PICKAXE

....

TRAIL

....

EMOTES

....

LOADOUT:

....

....

....

....

TACTICS:

....

....

....

....

....

KEY STATS:

TOTAL ELIMINATIONS IN ONE GAME

....

TOTAL ELIMINATIONS FOR THE DAY

....

FINAL PLACEMENTS

....

VICTORY ROYALES EARNED:

....

DATE:

....

IN-GAME TAG:

....

WHERE WE DROPPED IN:

....

....

....

SQUAD MEMBERS:

....

....

....

....

....

LOCKER:

OUTFIT

....

BACK BLING

....

PICKAXE

....

TRAIL

....

EMOTES

....

LOADOUT:

....

....

....

....

....

TACTICS:

....

....

....

....

....

KEY STATS:

TOTAL ELIMINATIONS IN ONE GAME

....

TOTAL ELIMINATIONS FOR THE DAY

....

FINAL PLACEMENTS

....

VICTORY ROYALES EARNED:

....

DATE:

....

IN-GAME TAG:

....

WHERE WE DROPPED IN:

....

....

....

SQUAD MEMBERS:

....

....

....

....

LOCKER:

OUTFIT

....

BACK BLING

....

PICKAXE

....

TRAIL

....

EMOTES

....

LOADOUT:

....

....

....

....

TACTICS:

....

....

....

....

....

KEY STATS:

TOTAL ELIMINATIONS IN ONE GAME

....

TOTAL ELIMINATIONS FOR THE DAY

....

FINAL PLACEMENTS

....

VICTORY ROYALES EARNED:

....

DATE:

....

IN-GAME TAG:

....

WHERE WE DROPPED IN:

....

....

SQUAD MEMBERS:

....

....

....

....

LOCKER:

OUTFIT

....

BACK BLING

....

PICKAXE

....

TRAIL

....

EMOTES

....

LOADOUT:

....

....

....

....

TACTICS:

....

....

....

....

....

KEY STATS:

TOTAL ELIMINATIONS IN ONE GAME

....

TOTAL ELIMINATIONS FOR THE DAY

....

FINAL PLACEMENTS

....

VICTORY ROYALES EARNED:

....

DATE:

....

IN-GAME TAG:

....

WHERE WE DROPPED IN:

....

....

SQUAD MEMBERS:

....

....

....

....

LOCKER:

OUTFIT

....

BACK BLING

....

PICKAXE

....

TRAIL

....

EMOTES

....

LOADOUT:

....

....

....

....

TACTICS:

....

....

....

....

....

KEY STATS:

TOTAL ELIMINATIONS IN ONE GAME

....

TOTAL ELIMINATIONS FOR THE DAY

....

FINAL PLACEMENTS

....

VICTORY ROYALES EARNED:

....

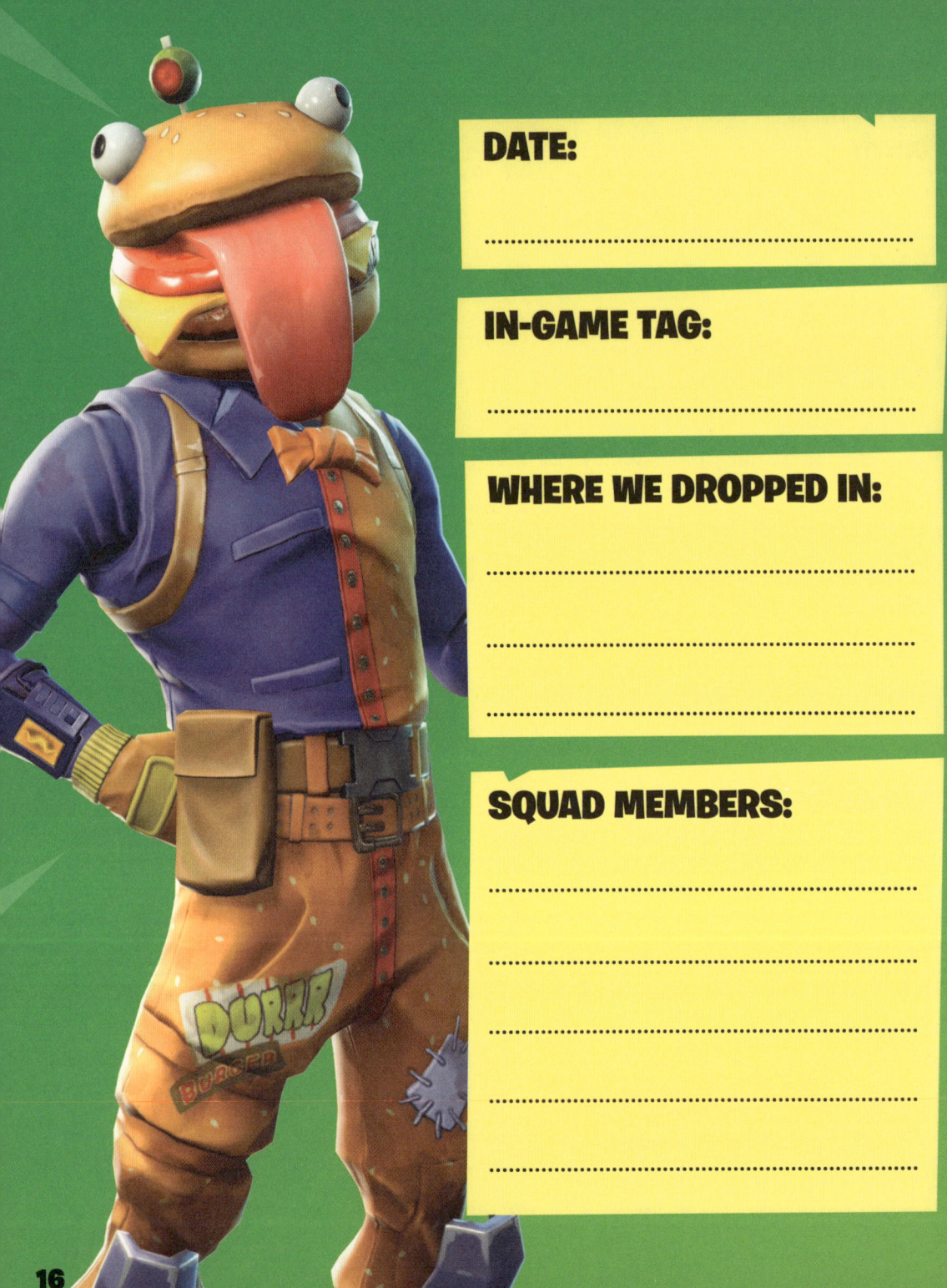

DATE:

....

IN-GAME TAG:

....

WHERE WE DROPPED IN:

....

....

....

SQUAD MEMBERS:

....

....

....

....

....

LOCKER:

OUTFIT

....

BACK BLING

....

PICKAXE

....

TRAIL

....

EMOTES

....

LOADOUT:

....

....

....

....

TACTICS:

....

....

....

....

....

KEY STATS:

TOTAL ELIMINATIONS IN ONE GAME

....

TOTAL ELIMINATIONS FOR THE DAY

....

FINAL PLACEMENTS

....

VICTORY ROYALES EARNED:

....

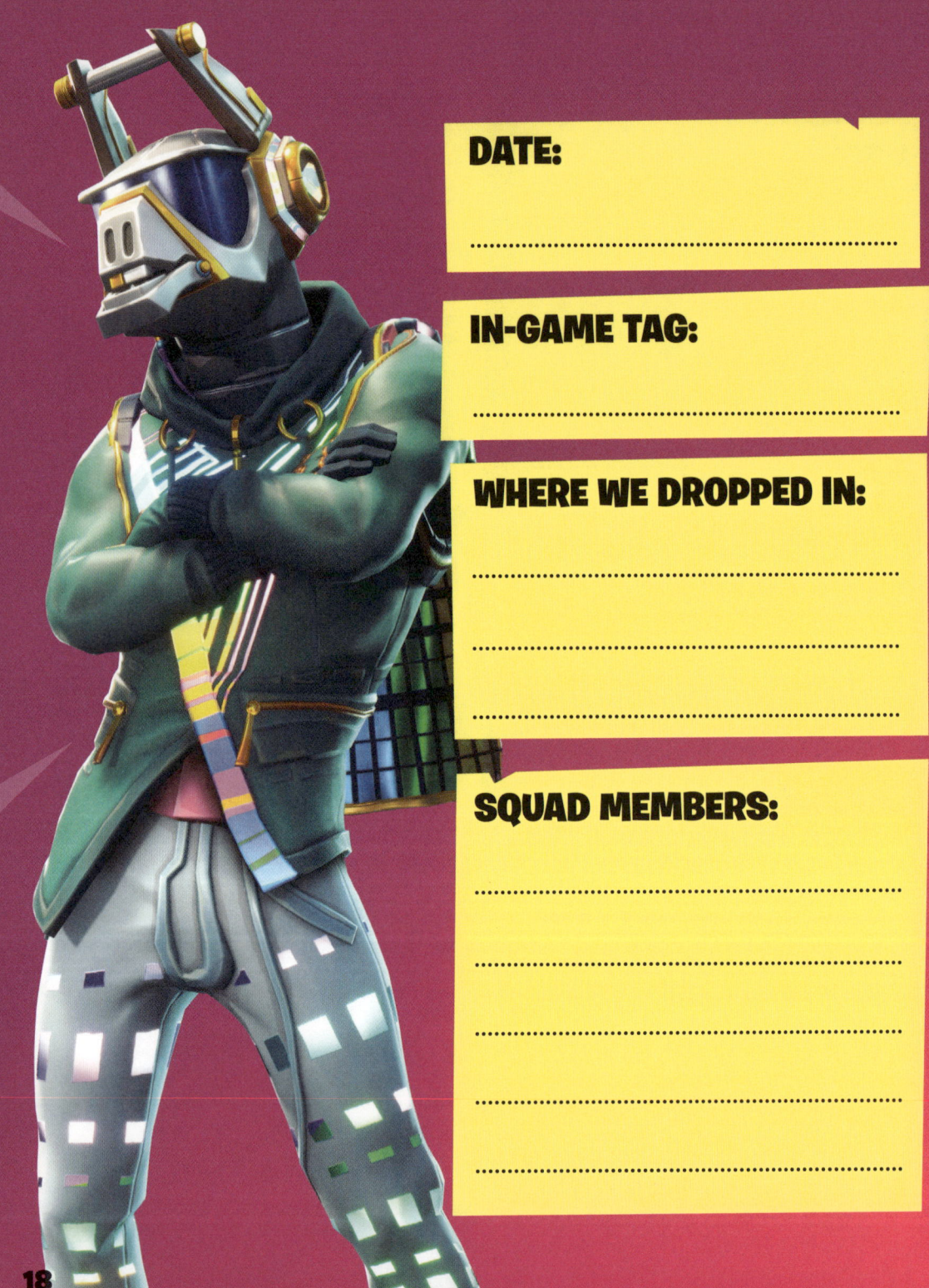

DATE:

....

IN-GAME TAG:

....

WHERE WE DROPPED IN:

....

....

....

SQUAD MEMBERS:

....

....

....

....

LOCKER:

OUTFIT

....

BACK BLING

....

PICKAXE

....

TRAIL

....

EMOTES

....

LOADOUT:

....

....

....

....

....

TACTICS:

....

....

....

....

....

KEY STATS:

TOTAL ELIMINATIONS IN ONE GAME

....

TOTAL ELIMINATIONS FOR THE DAY

....

FINAL PLACEMENTS

....

VICTORY ROYALES EARNED:

....

DATE:

....

IN-GAME TAG:

....

WHERE WE DROPPED IN:

....

....

....

SQUAD MEMBERS:

....

....

....

....

....

LOCKER:

OUTFIT

....

BACK BLING

....

PICKAXE

....

TRAIL

....

EMOTES

....

LOADOUT:

....

....

....

....

TACTICS:

....

....

....

....

....

KEY STATS:

TOTAL ELIMINATIONS IN ONE GAME

....

TOTAL ELIMINATIONS FOR THE DAY

....

FINAL PLACEMENTS

....

VICTORY ROYALES EARNED:

....

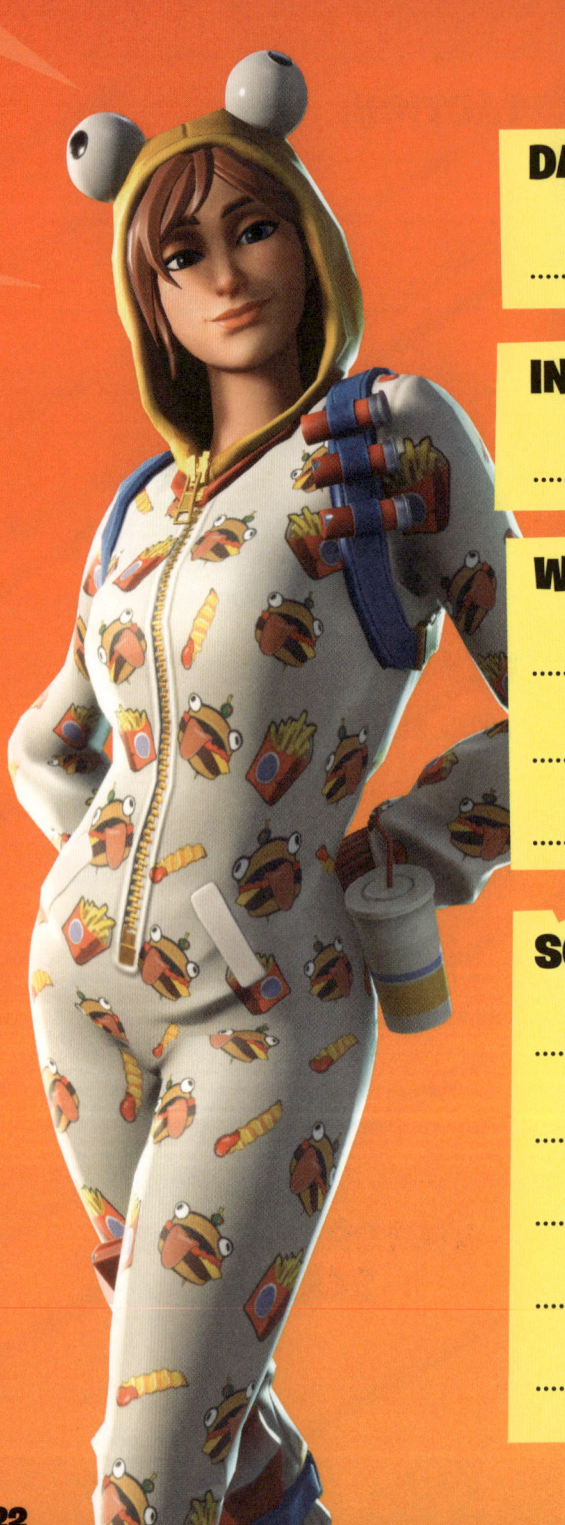

DATE:

....

IN-GAME TAG:

....

WHERE WE DROPPED IN:

....

....

....

SQUAD MEMBERS:

....

....

....

....

LOCKER:

OUTFIT

....

BACK BLING

....

PICKAXE

....

TRAIL

....

EMOTES

....

LOADOUT:

....

....

....

....

TACTICS:

....

....

....

....

....

KEY STATS:

TOTAL ELIMINATIONS IN ONE GAME

....

TOTAL ELIMINATIONS FOR THE DAY

....

FINAL PLACEMENTS

....

VICTORY ROYALES EARNED:

....

DATE:

....

IN-GAME TAG:

....

WHERE WE DROPPED IN:

....
....
....

SQUAD MEMBERS:

....
....
....
....

LOCKER:

OUTFIT

....

BACK BLING

....

PICKAXE

....

TRAIL

....

EMOTES

....

LOADOUT:

....

....

....

....

TACTICS:

....

....

....

....

....

KEY STATS:

TOTAL ELIMINATIONS IN ONE GAME

....

TOTAL ELIMINATIONS FOR THE DAY

....

FINAL PLACEMENTS

....

VICTORY ROYALES EARNED:

....

DATE:

....

IN-GAME TAG:

....

WHERE WE DROPPED IN:

....

....

....

SQUAD MEMBERS:

....

....

....

....

....

LOCKER:

OUTFIT

....

BACK BLING

....

PICKAXE

....

TRAIL

....

EMOTES

....

LOADOUT:

....

....

....

....

TACTICS:

....

....

....

....

....

KEY STATS:

TOTAL ELIMINATIONS IN ONE GAME

....

TOTAL ELIMINATIONS FOR THE DAY

....

FINAL PLACEMENTS

....

VICTORY ROYALES EARNED:

....

27

DATE:

....

IN-GAME TAG:

....

WHERE WE DROPPED IN:

....

....

....

SQUAD MEMBERS:

....

....

....

....

....

LOCKER:

OUTFIT

....

BACK BLING

....

PICKAXE

....

TRAIL

....

EMOTES

....

LOADOUT:

....

....

....

....

....

TACTICS:

....

....

....

....

....

KEY STATS:

TOTAL ELIMINATIONS IN ONE GAME

....

TOTAL ELIMINATIONS FOR THE DAY

....

FINAL PLACEMENTS

....

VICTORY ROYALES EARNED:

....

DATE:

....

IN-GAME TAG:

....

WHERE WE DROPPED IN:

....

....

....

SQUAD MEMBERS:

....

....

....

....

LOCKER:

OUTFIT

....

BACK BLING

....

PICKAXE

....

TRAIL

....

EMOTES

....

LOADOUT:

....

....

....

....

TACTICS:

....

....

....

....

....

KEY STATS:

TOTAL ELIMINATIONS IN ONE GAME

....

TOTAL ELIMINATIONS FOR THE DAY

....

FINAL PLACEMENTS

....

VICTORY ROYALES EARNED:

....

DATE:

....

IN-GAME TAG:

....

WHERE WE DROPPED IN:

....

....

....

SQUAD MEMBERS:

....

....

....

....

LOCKER:

OUTFIT

....

BACK BLING

....

PICKAXE

....

TRAIL

....

EMOTES

....

LOADOUT:

....

....

....

....

TACTICS:

....

....

....

....

....

KEY STATS:

TOTAL ELIMINATIONS IN ONE GAME

....

TOTAL ELIMINATIONS FOR THE DAY

....

FINAL PLACEMENTS

....

VICTORY ROYALES EARNED:

....

DATE:

....

IN-GAME TAG:

....

WHERE WE DROPPED IN:

....

....

....

SQUAD MEMBERS:

....

....

....

....

....

LOCKER:

OUTFIT

....

BACK BLING

....

PICKAXE

....

TRAIL

....

EMOTES

....

LOADOUT:

....

....

....

....

TACTICS:

....

....

....

....

....

KEY STATS:

TOTAL ELIMINATIONS IN ONE GAME

....

TOTAL ELIMINATIONS FOR THE DAY

....

FINAL PLACEMENTS

....

VICTORY ROYALES EARNED:

....

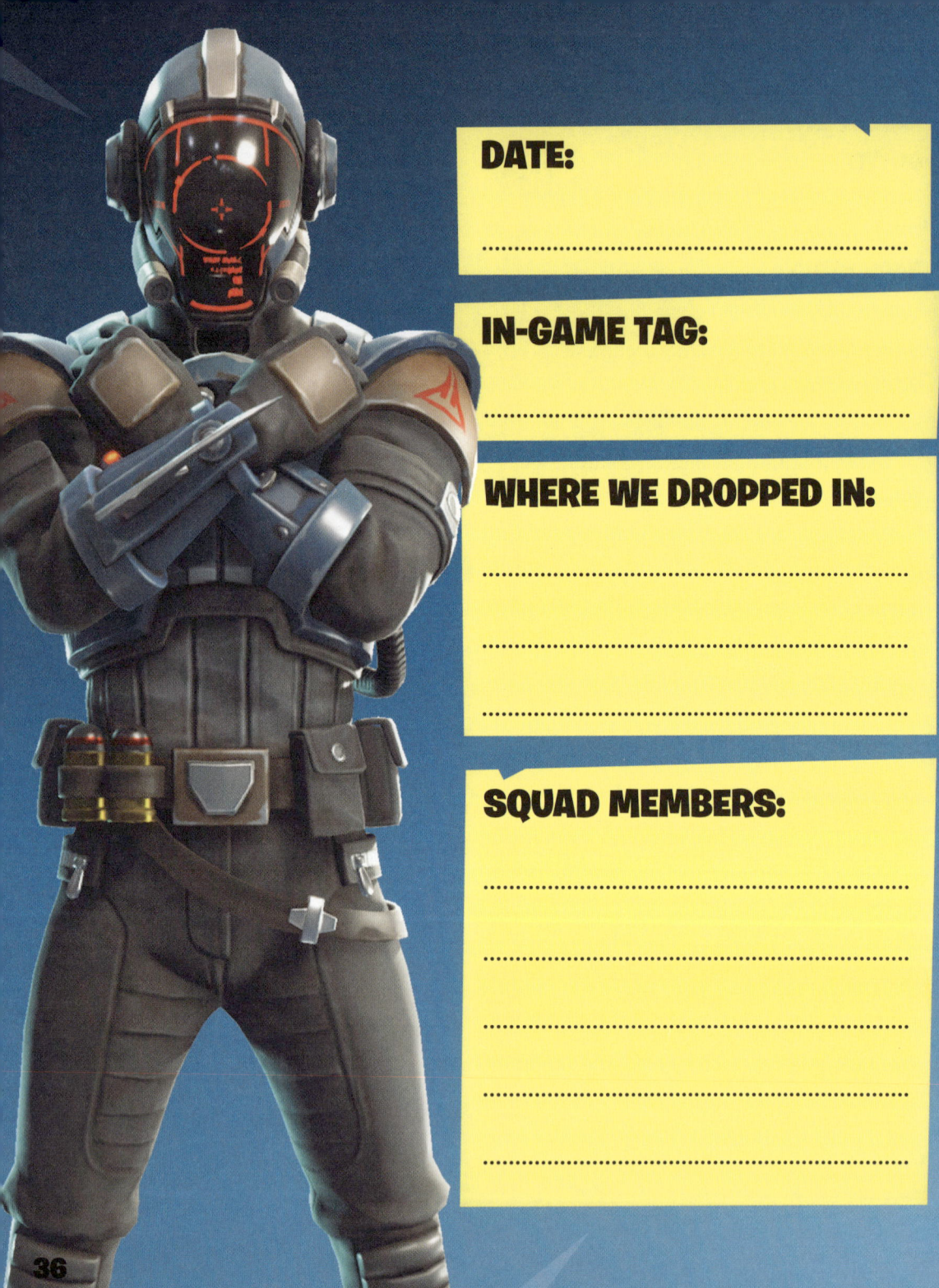

DATE:

....

IN-GAME TAG:

....

WHERE WE DROPPED IN:

....

....

....

SQUAD MEMBERS:

....

....

....

....

....

LOCKER:

OUTFIT

....

BACK BLING

....

PICKAXE

....

TRAIL

....

EMOTES

....

LOADOUT:

....

....

....

....

....

TACTICS:

....

....

....

....

....

KEY STATS:

TOTAL ELIMINATIONS IN ONE GAME

....

TOTAL ELIMINATIONS FOR THE DAY

....

FINAL PLACEMENTS

....

VICTORY ROYALES EARNED:

....

DATE:

....

IN-GAME TAG:

....

WHERE WE DROPPED IN:

....

....

....

SQUAD MEMBERS:

....

....

....

....

LOCKER:

OUTFIT

·····································

BACK BLING

·····································

PICKAXE

·····································

TRAIL

·····································

EMOTES

·····································

LOADOUT:

·····································

·····································

·····································

·····································

·····································

TACTICS:

·····································

·····································

·····································

·····································

·····································

KEY STATS:

TOTAL ELIMINATIONS IN ONE GAME

·····································

TOTAL ELIMINATIONS FOR THE DAY

·····································

FINAL PLACEMENTS

·····································

VICTORY ROYALES EARNED:

·····································

DATE:

....

IN-GAME TAG:

....

WHERE WE DROPPED IN:

....

....

....

SQUAD MEMBERS:

....

....

....

....

....

LOCKER:

OUTFIT

....

BACK BLING

....

PICKAXE

....

TRAIL

....

EMOTES

....

LOADOUT:

....

....

....

....

TACTICS:

....

....

....

....

....

KEY STATS:

TOTAL ELIMINATIONS IN ONE GAME

....

TOTAL ELIMINATIONS FOR THE DAY

....

FINAL PLACEMENTS

....

VICTORY ROYALES EARNED:

....

DATE:

....

IN-GAME TAG:

....

WHERE WE DROPPED IN:

....

....

....

SQUAD MEMBERS:

....

....

....

....

....

LOCKER:

OUTFIT

....

BACK BLING

....

PICKAXE

....

TRAIL

....

EMOTES

....

LOADOUT:

....

....

....

....

TACTICS:

....

....

....

....

....

KEY STATS:

TOTAL ELIMINATIONS IN ONE GAME

....

TOTAL ELIMINATIONS FOR THE DAY

....

FINAL PLACEMENTS

....

VICTORY ROYALES EARNED:

....

43

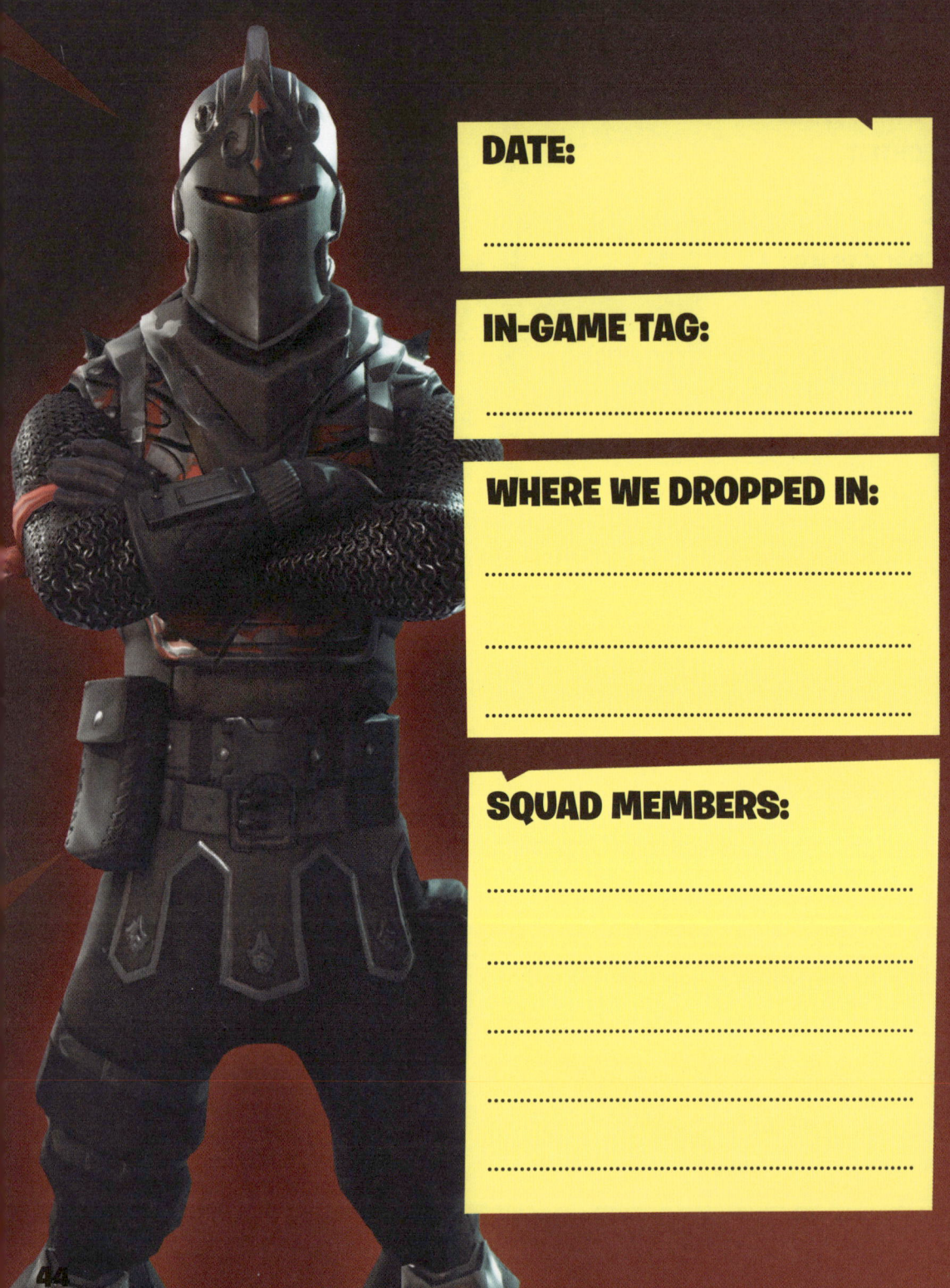

DATE:

....

IN-GAME TAG:

....

WHERE WE DROPPED IN:

....

....

....

SQUAD MEMBERS:

....

....

....

....

LOCKER:

OUTFIT

....

BACK BLING

....

PICKAXE

....

TRAIL

....

EMOTES

....

LOADOUT:

....

....

....

....

....

TACTICS:

....

....

....

....

....

KEY STATS:

TOTAL ELIMINATIONS IN ONE GAME

....

TOTAL ELIMINATIONS FOR THE DAY

....

FINAL PLACEMENTS

....

VICTORY ROYALES EARNED:

....

45

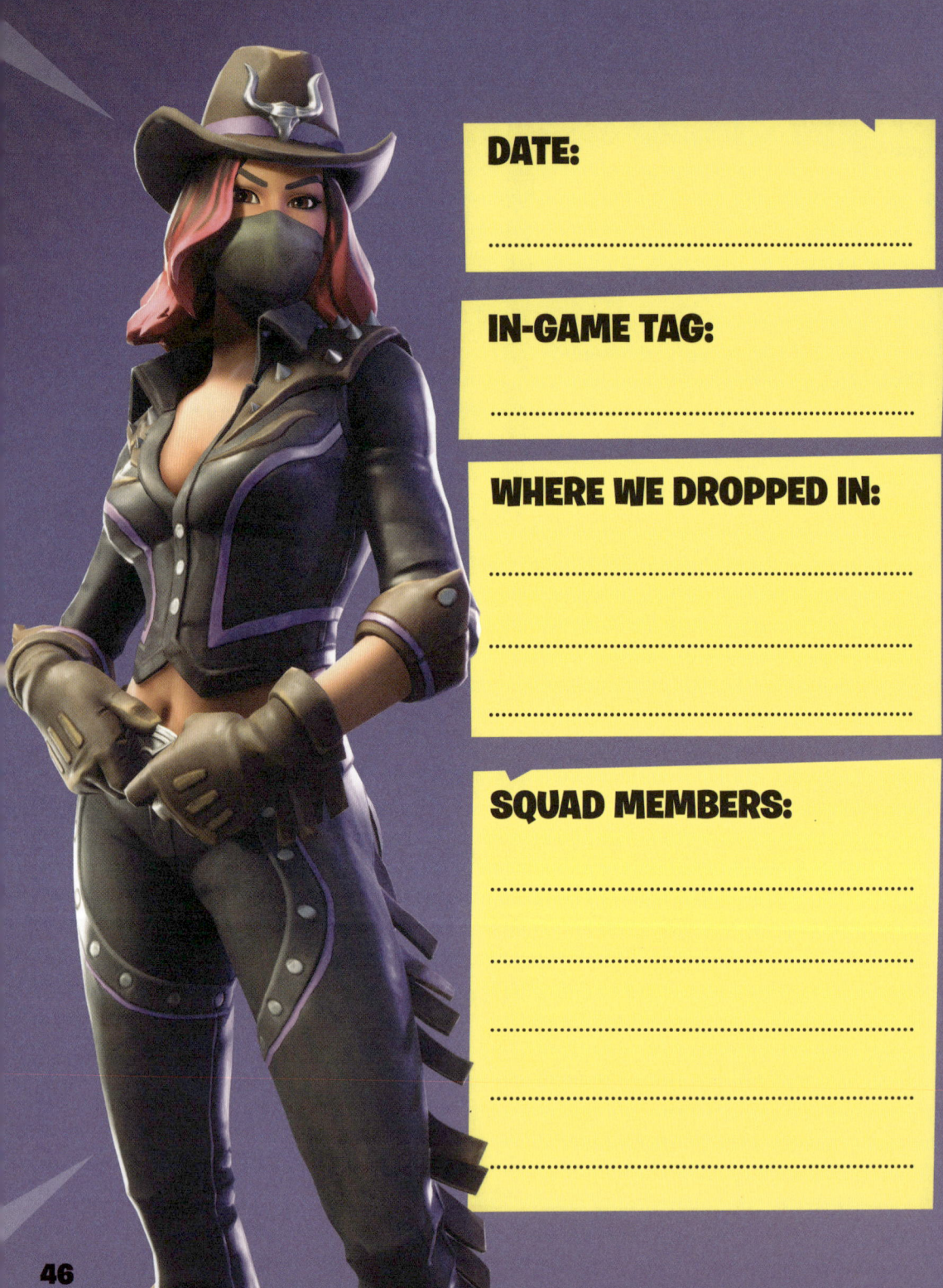

DATE:

....

IN-GAME TAG:

....

WHERE WE DROPPED IN:

....

....

....

SQUAD MEMBERS:

....

....

....

....

LOCKER:

OUTFIT

....

BACK BLING

....

PICKAXE

....

TRAIL

....

EMOTES

....

LOADOUT:

....

....

....

....

TACTICS:

....

....

....

....

....

....

KEY STATS:

TOTAL ELIMINATIONS IN ONE GAME

....

TOTAL ELIMINATIONS FOR THE DAY

....

FINAL PLACEMENTS

....

VICTORY ROYALES EARNED:

....

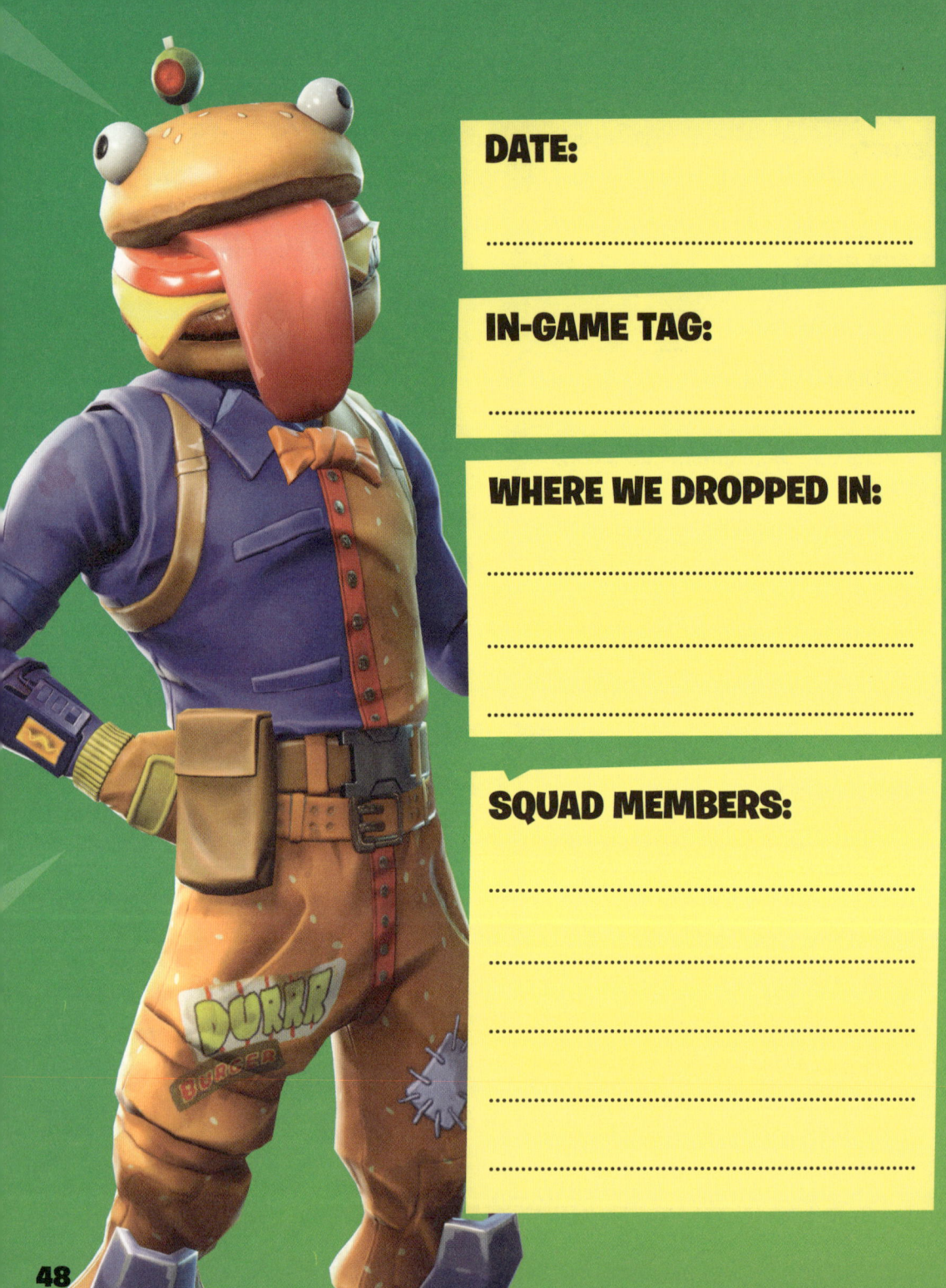

DATE:

....

IN-GAME TAG:

....

WHERE WE DROPPED IN:

....

....

....

SQUAD MEMBERS:

....

....

....

....

....

LOCKER:

OUTFIT

....

BACK BLING

....

PICKAXE

....

TRAIL

....

EMOTES

....

LOADOUT:

....

....

....

....

TACTICS:

....

....

....

....

....

KEY STATS:

TOTAL ELIMINATIONS IN ONE GAME

....

TOTAL ELIMINATIONS FOR THE DAY

....

FINAL PLACEMENTS

....

VICTORY ROYALES EARNED:

....

DATE:

....

IN-GAME TAG:

....

WHERE WE DROPPED IN:

....

....

....

SQUAD MEMBERS:

....

....

....

....

LOCKER:

OUTFIT

....

BACK BLING

....

PICKAXE

....

TRAIL

....

EMOTES

....

LOADOUT:

....

....

....

....

....

TACTICS:

....

....

....

....

....

KEY STATS:

TOTAL ELIMINATIONS IN ONE GAME

....

TOTAL ELIMINATIONS FOR THE DAY

....

FINAL PLACEMENTS

....

VICTORY ROYALES EARNED:

....

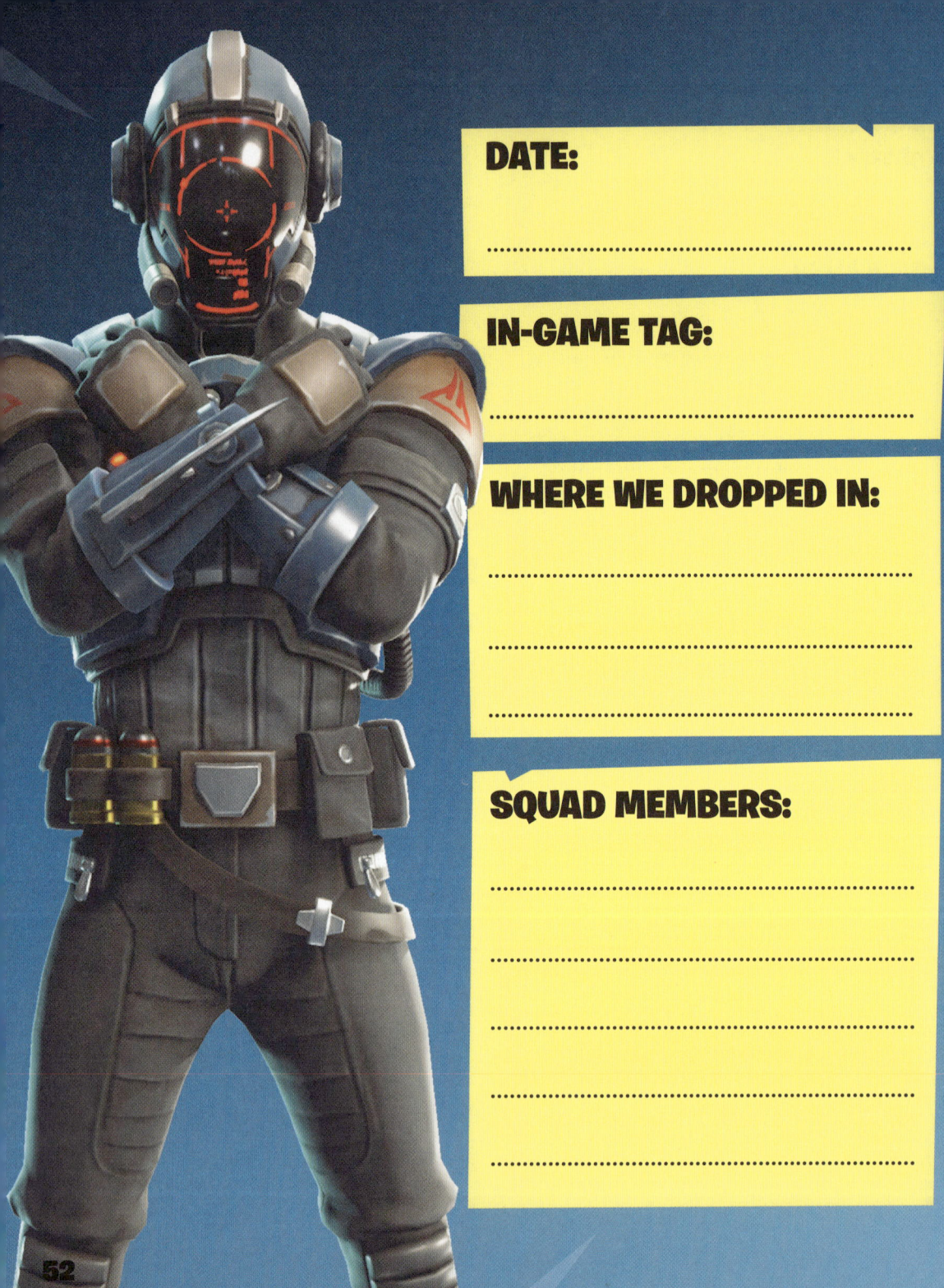

DATE:

....

IN-GAME TAG:

....

WHERE WE DROPPED IN:

....

....

....

SQUAD MEMBERS:

....

....

....

....

....

LOCKER:

OUTFIT

....

BACK BLING

....

PICKAXE

....

TRAIL

....

EMOTES

....

LOADOUT:

....

....

....

....

....

TACTICS:

....

....

....

....

....

KEY STATS:

TOTAL ELIMINATIONS IN ONE GAME

....

TOTAL ELIMINATIONS FOR THE DAY

....

FINAL PLACEMENTS

....

VICTORY ROYALES EARNED:

....

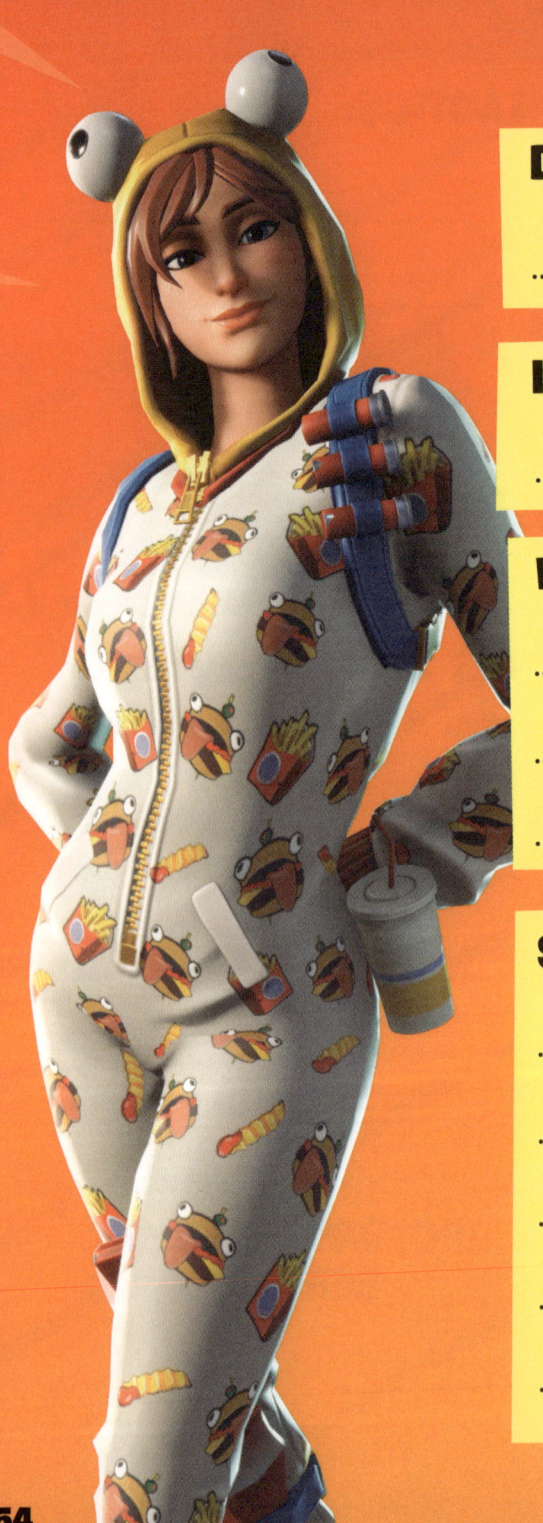

DATE:

....

IN-GAME TAG:

....

WHERE WE DROPPED IN:

....

....

....

SQUAD MEMBERS:

....

....

....

....

....

LOCKER:

OUTFIT

....

BACK BLING

....

PICKAXE

....

TRAIL

....

EMOTES

....

LOADOUT:

....

....

....

....

TACTICS:

....

....

....

....

....

KEY STATS:

TOTAL ELIMINATIONS IN ONE GAME

....

TOTAL ELIMINATIONS FOR THE DAY

....

FINAL PLACEMENTS

....

VICTORY ROYALES EARNED:

....

DATE:

....

IN-GAME TAG:

....

WHERE WE DROPPED IN:

....

....

....

SQUAD MEMBERS:

....

....

....

....

....

LOCKER:

OUTFIT

....

BACK BLING

....

PICKAXE

....

TRAIL

....

EMOTES

....

LOADOUT:

....

....

....

....

TACTICS:

....

....

....

....

....

KEY STATS:

TOTAL ELIMINATIONS IN ONE GAME

....

TOTAL ELIMINATIONS FOR THE DAY

....

FINAL PLACEMENTS

....

VICTORY ROYALES EARNED:

....

DATE:

....

IN-GAME TAG:

....

WHERE WE DROPPED IN:

....

....

....

SQUAD MEMBERS:

....

....

....

....

....

LOCKER:

OUTFIT

....

BACK BLING

....

PICKAXE

....

TRAIL

....

EMOTES

....

LOADOUT:

....

....

....

....

....

TACTICS:

....

....

....

....

....

KEY STATS:

TOTAL ELIMINATIONS IN ONE GAME

....

TOTAL ELIMINATIONS FOR THE DAY

....

FINAL PLACEMENTS

....

VICTORY ROYALES EARNED:

....

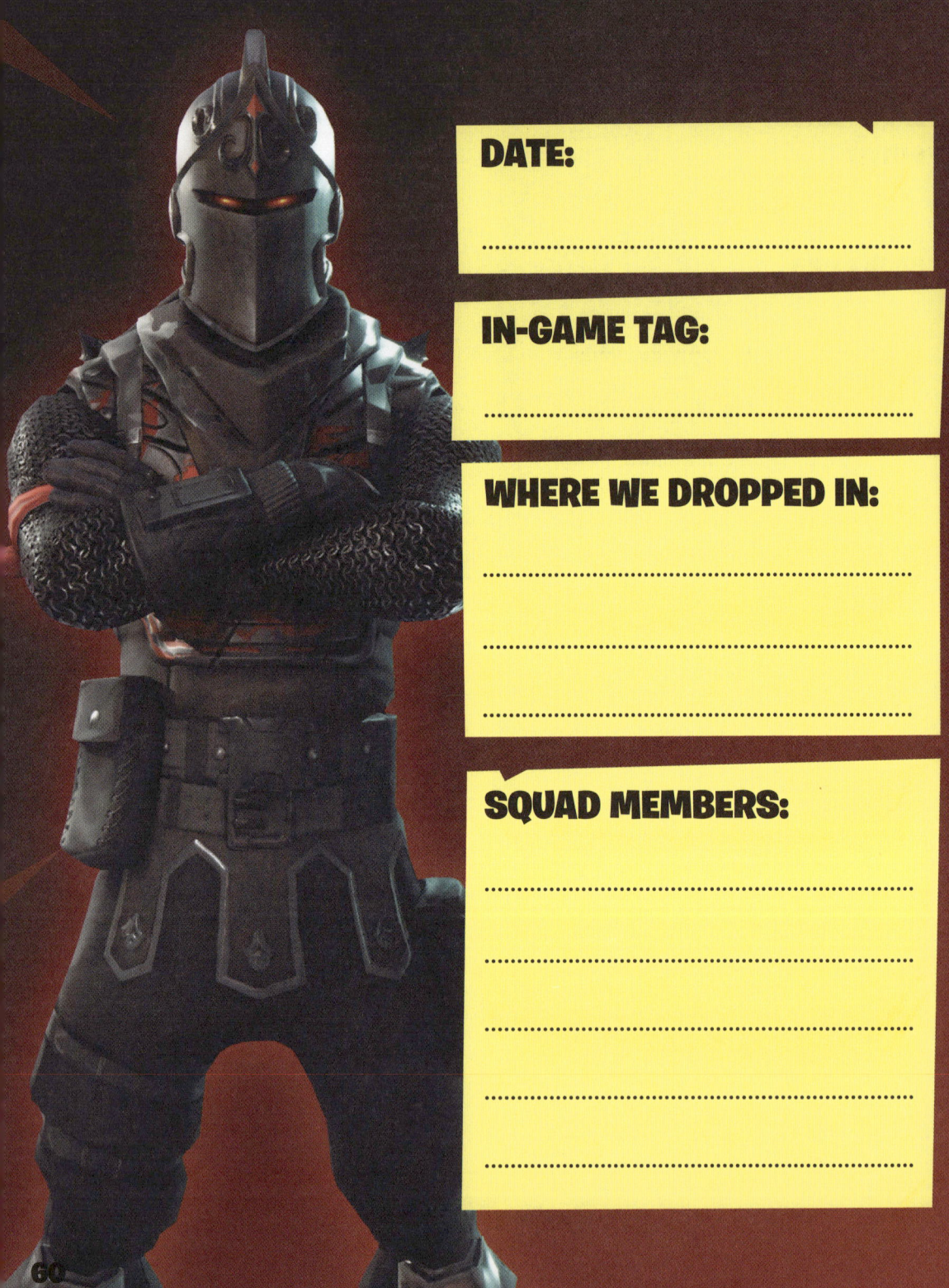

DATE:

....

IN-GAME TAG:

....

WHERE WE DROPPED IN:

....

....

....

SQUAD MEMBERS:

....

....

....

....

....

LOCKER:

OUTFIT

....

BACK BLING

....

PICKAXE

....

TRAIL

....

EMOTES

....

LOADOUT:

....

....

....

....

....

TACTICS:

....

....

....

....

....

KEY STATS:

TOTAL ELIMINATIONS IN ONE GAME

....

TOTAL ELIMINATIONS FOR THE DAY

....

FINAL PLACEMENTS

....

VICTORY ROYALES EARNED:

....

DATE:

....

IN-GAME TAG:

....

WHERE WE DROPPED IN:

....

....

....

SQUAD MEMBERS:

....

....

....

....

LOCKER:

OUTFIT

....

BACK BLING

....

PICKAXE

....

TRAIL

....

EMOTES

....

LOADOUT:

....

....

....

....

TACTICS:

....

....

....

....

....

KEY STATS:

TOTAL ELIMINATIONS IN ONE GAME

....

TOTAL ELIMINATIONS FOR THE DAY

....

FINAL PLACEMENTS

....

VICTORY ROYALES EARNED:

....

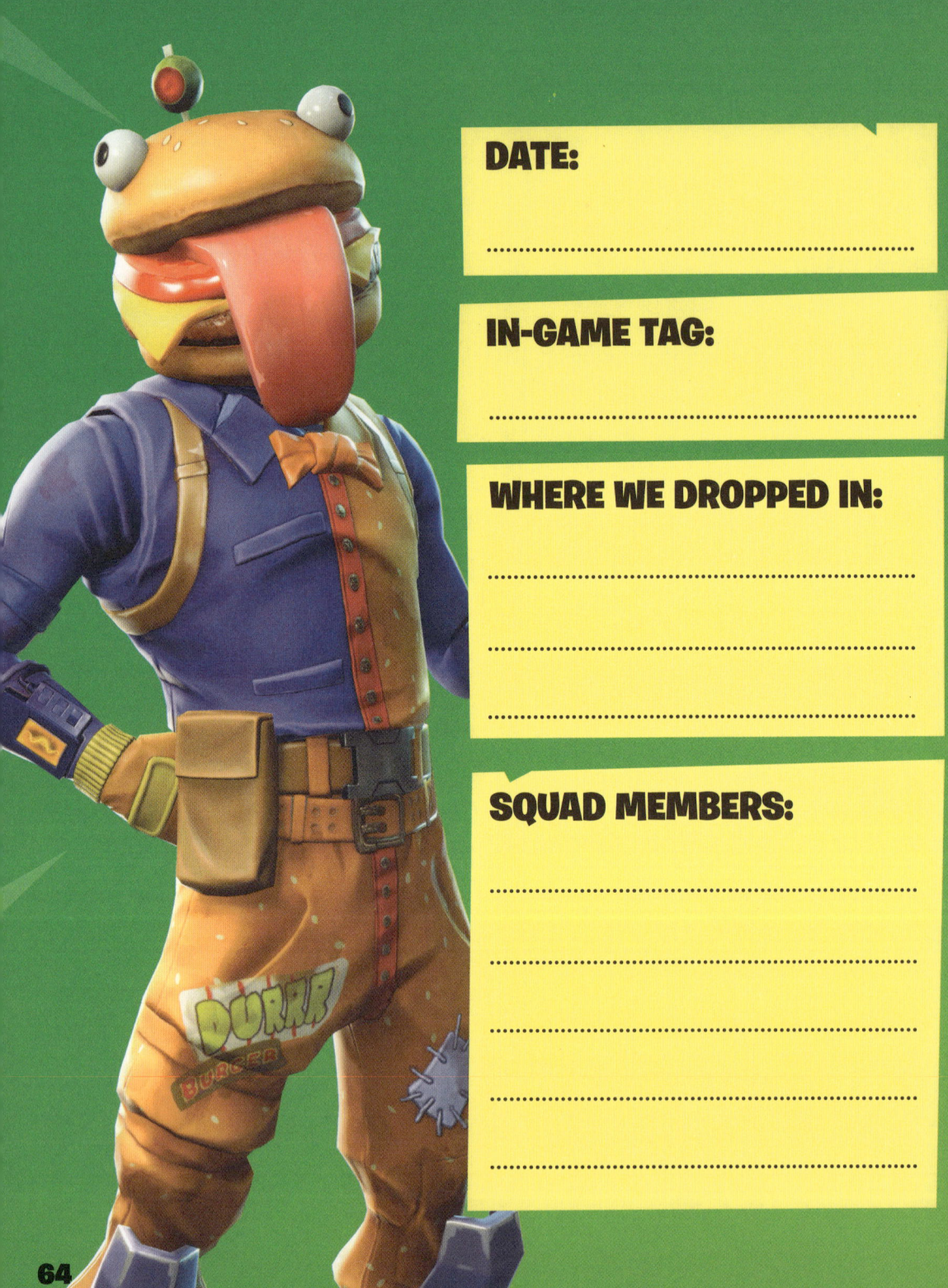

DATE:

....

IN-GAME TAG:

....

WHERE WE DROPPED IN:

....

....

....

SQUAD MEMBERS:

....

....

....

....

LOCKER:

OUTFIT

....

BACK BLING

....

PICKAXE

....

TRAIL

....

EMOTES

....

LOADOUT:

....

....

....

....

TACTICS:

....

....

....

....

....

KEY STATS:

TOTAL ELIMINATIONS IN ONE GAME

....

TOTAL ELIMINATIONS FOR THE DAY

....

FINAL PLACEMENTS

....

VICTORY ROYALES EARNED:

....

DATE:

....

IN-GAME TAG:

....

WHERE WE DROPPED IN:

....

....

....

SQUAD MEMBERS:

....

....

....

....

....

LOCKER:

OUTFIT

....

BACK BLING

....

PICKAXE

....

TRAIL

....

EMOTES

....

LOADOUT:

....

....

....

....

....

TACTICS:

....

....

....

....

....

KEY STATS:

TOTAL ELIMINATIONS IN ONE GAME

....

TOTAL ELIMINATIONS FOR THE DAY

....

FINAL PLACEMENTS

....

VICTORY ROYALES EARNED:

....

DATE:
....

IN-GAME TAG:
....

WHERE WE DROPPED IN:
....
....
....

SQUAD MEMBERS:
....
....
....
....

LOCKER:

OUTFIT

....

BACK BLING

....

PICKAXE

....

TRAIL

....

EMOTES

....

LOADOUT:

....

....

....

....

....

TACTICS:

....

....

....

....

....

KEY STATS:

TOTAL ELIMINATIONS IN ONE GAME

....

TOTAL ELIMINATIONS FOR THE DAY

....

FINAL PLACEMENTS

....

VICTORY ROYALES EARNED:

....

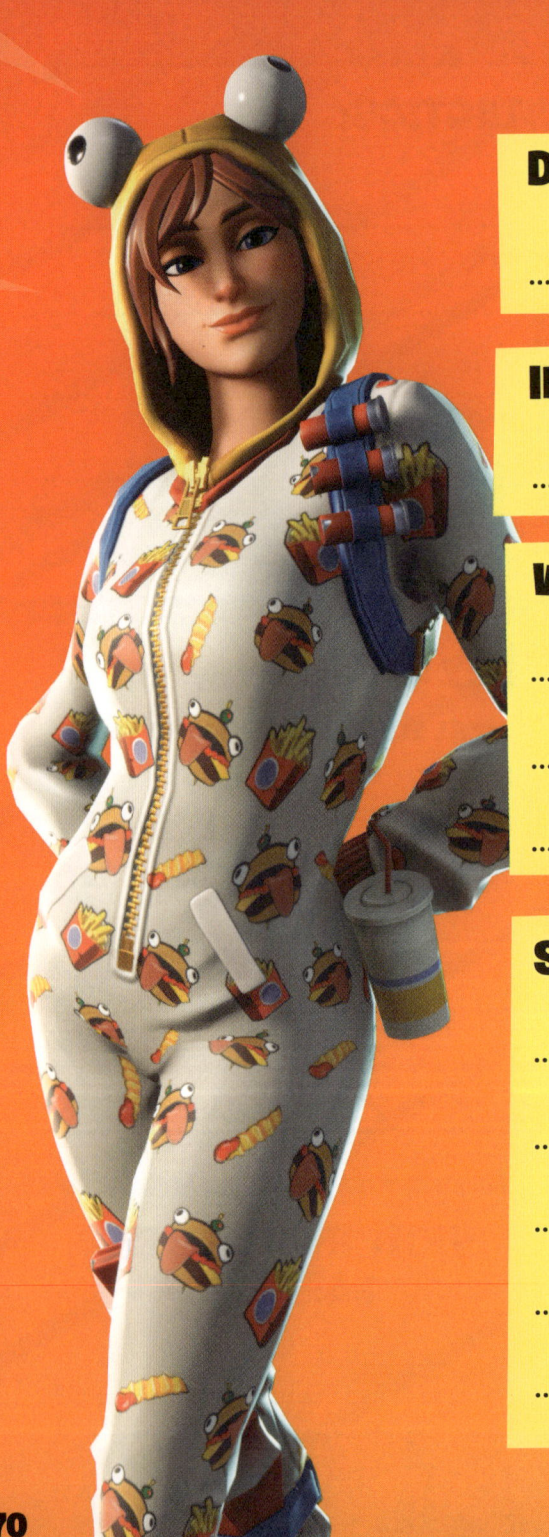

DATE:

....

IN-GAME TAG:

....

WHERE WE DROPPED IN:

....

....

....

SQUAD MEMBERS:

....

....

....

....

....

LOCKER:

OUTFIT

....

BACK BLING

....

PICKAXE

....

TRAIL

....

EMOTES

....

LOADOUT:

....

....

....

....

TACTICS:

....

....

....

....

....

KEY STATS:

TOTAL ELIMINATIONS IN ONE GAME

....

TOTAL ELIMINATIONS FOR THE DAY

....

FINAL PLACEMENTS

....

VICTORY ROYALES EARNED:

....

DATE:

....

IN-GAME TAG:

....

WHERE WE DROPPED IN:

....

....

....

SQUAD MEMBERS:

....

....

....

....

LOCKER:

OUTFIT

....

BACK BLING

....

PICKAXE

....

TRAIL

....

EMOTES

....

LOADOUT:

....

....

....

....

....

TACTICS:

....

....

....

....

....

KEY STATS:

TOTAL ELIMINATIONS IN ONE GAME

....

TOTAL ELIMINATIONS FOR THE DAY

....

FINAL PLACEMENTS

....

VICTORY ROYALES EARNED:

....

DATE:

....

IN-GAME TAG:

....

WHERE WE DROPPED IN:

....

....

....

SQUAD MEMBERS:

....

....

....

....

LOCKER:

OUTFIT

....

BACK BLING

....

PICKAXE

....

TRAIL

....

EMOTES

....

LOADOUT:

....

....

....

....

....

TACTICS:

....

....

....

....

....

KEY STATS:

TOTAL ELIMINATIONS IN ONE GAME

....

TOTAL ELIMINATIONS FOR THE DAY

....

FINAL PLACEMENTS

....

VICTORY ROYALES EARNED:

....

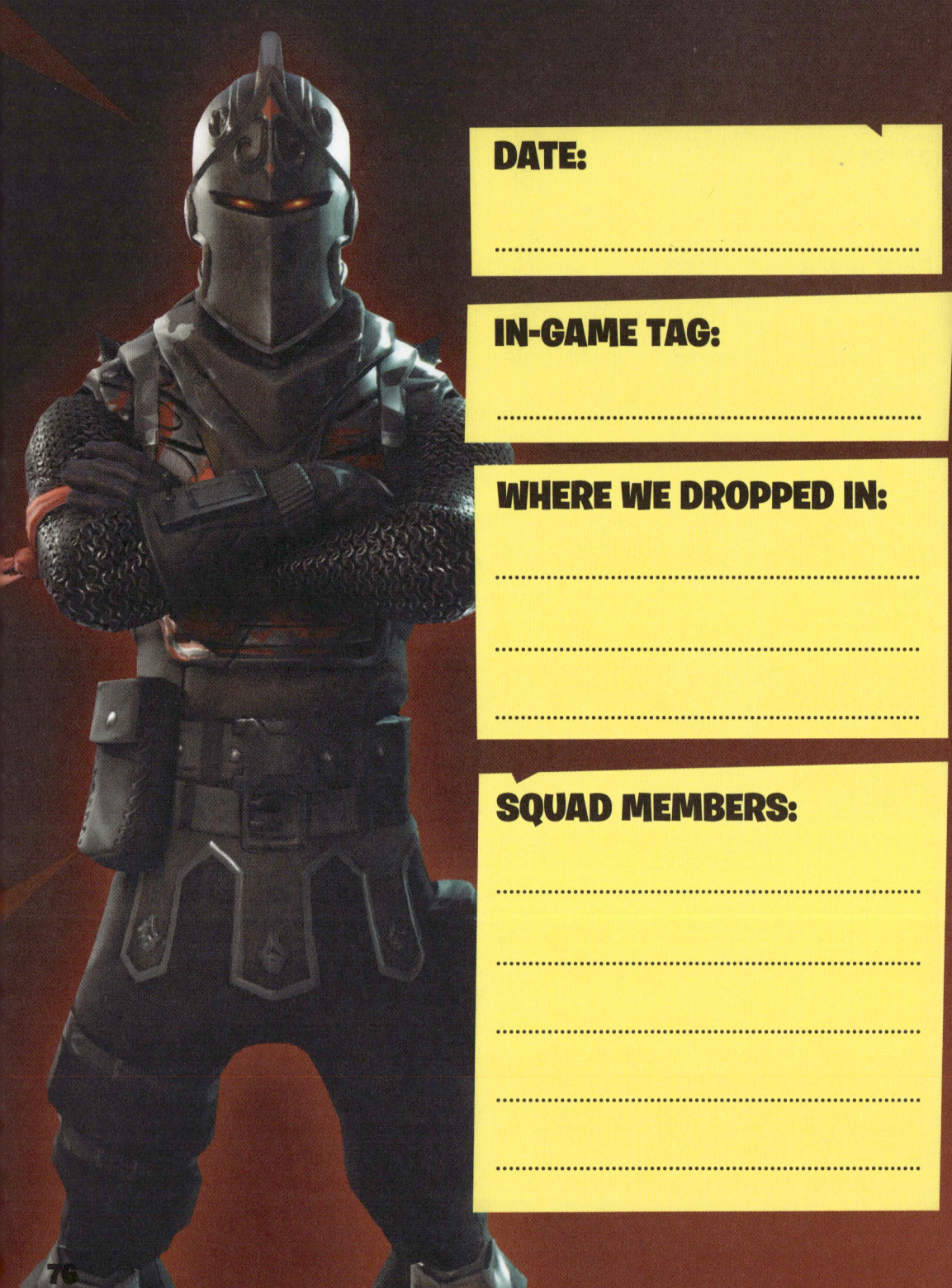

DATE:

....

IN-GAME TAG:

....

WHERE WE DROPPED IN:

....

....

....

SQUAD MEMBERS:

....

....

....

....

LOCKER:

OUTFIT

....

BACK BLING

....

PICKAXE

....

TRAIL

....

EMOTES

....

LOADOUT:

....

....

....

....

TACTICS:

....

....

....

....

....

KEY STATS:

TOTAL ELIMINATIONS IN ONE GAME

....

TOTAL ELIMINATIONS FOR THE DAY

....

FINAL PLACEMENTS

....

VICTORY ROYALES EARNED:

....

IN THE LOCKER

OUTFITS I HAVE:

OUTFITS I WANT:

EMOTES I HAVE:

EMOTES I WANT:

ITEMS I HAVE:
(BACK BLING, HARVESTING TOOLS, PETS, GLIDERS, ETC.)

ITEMS I WANT:
(BACK BLING, HARVESTING TOOLS, PETS, GLIDERS, ETC.)

CREATE YOUR OWN OUTFITS

NAME: ....

NAME: ....

NAME: ....

NAME: ....

NAME: ....

NAME: ....

NAME: ....

NAME: ....

CREATE YOUR OWN WEAPONS

NAME: ....

NAME: ....

NAME: ....

NAME: ....

NAME: ....

NAME: ....

NAME: ....

NAME: ....

FIELD NOTES/STRATEGIES:

FIELD NOTES/STRATEGIES:

....
....
....
....
....
....
....
....
....
....
....
....
....
....
....
....
....
....